Stressbusters

For Moms

Deborah Shaw Lewis

Stressbusters

For Moms

MOTHERS OF
M♥PS.
PRESCHOOLERS

ZondervanPublishingHouse
Grand Rapids, Michigan

A Division of HarperCollinsPublishers

Stressbusters for Moms
Copyright © 1996 by Deborah Shaw Lewis

Requests for information should be addressed to:
ZondervanPublishingHouse
Grand Rapids, Michigan 49530

Library of Congress Cataloging-in-Publication Data

Lewis, Deborah Shaw, 1951–
    Stressbusters for moms / Deborah Shaw Lewis.
        p.   cm.
    ISBN: 0-310-20566-2 (softcover : alk. paper)
    1. Motherhood—Psychological aspects—Miscellanea.   2. Stress management—Miscellanea.
I. Title.
HQ759.L488 1996
306.874'3-dc20   5-48932
                                                                                                           CIP

All Scripture quotations, unless otherwise indicated, are taken from the *Holy Bible: New International Version*®. NIV®. Copyright © 1973, 1978, 1984 by International Bible Society. Used by permission of Zondervan Publishing House. All rights reserved.

Edited by Mary McNeil
Interior design by Sue Koppenol

Printed in the United States of America

---

96 97 98 99 00 01 02 /❖ EP/ 10 9 8 7 6 5 4 3 2

To my sisters and brothers:
Janice, Joan, Terrell, Carol, Beth, and David, who have
always had encouraging words of wisdom for me as a mother.

Introduction

Whenever I speak on the topic of motherhood stress, I close with a time for my listeners to share motherhood wisdom. Each time many of the same ideas come up: eat right; get exercise; talk to other mothers; enjoy your baby. And yet every time, someone shares an idea I've never heard before.

So I began collecting these stressbusters for moms. Some came from group discussions after Motherhood Stress workshops. Others came from letters written to me by women who read my book, *Motherhood Stress.* Some are from my experience with my five children.

I also sent out letters to dozens of friends. I asked them to answer four questions and to pass copies of the questionnaire to some of their acquaintances.

The questions were simple: What mothering advice would you give your sister? What stresses have you had lately, and how did you cope? What's the worst motherhood advice anyone ever gave you? Tell about a time you survived motherhood stress.

The answers were wonderful. Reading them was like attending a convention of mothers, each giving support, encouragement, and practical ideas for this high calling of motherhood. I wish I could have included them all.

Read this book as if it were a support group meeting. These ideas come from real women, each with her own mothering style. These ideas worked for the mothers who shared them with me. Some will work for you. Others may not fit your style of mothering or the needs of your child.

Laugh—or groan—at the stress-producing "worst advice." Isn't it amazing what people tell mothers to do? In reading the "motherhood stress moment" stories, I hope you will see yourself reflected and realize that you are not alone.

Most of all, I hope that you will find in these pages encouragement and strength to be the best mother you can be. In that there is much joy.

Deborah Shaw Lewis

STRESSBUSTER #1

Sing to and with your children. It's hard to be upset when you are singing.

C. G., mother of three, ages 21, 26, 29

STRESSBUSTER #2

Make rest a priority: nap *whenever* you can!

J. S., mother of two, ages 12, 15

STRESSBUSTER #3

Build close friendships with one or two other mothers. Talk to each other, do things together, and help each other out. Having another adult around keeps you sane and is more fun.

D. S., mother of four, ages 12, 16, 17, 19

Worst Motherhood Advice I Ever Heard

"Leave the baby in the crib when it cries. Nothing *you* do will stop it anyway."

S. T., mother of three, ages 2 months, 3, 5

STRESSBUSTER #4

Take care of yourself! When you do, you are saying, "I am valuable. I am the only mother my children will ever have. I need to be at my best for my children and my husband."

Deborah

STRESSBUSTER #5

Relax! That's the very good news about being a good parent. We can relax about many of the nonessentials. Don't worry about what your neighbors, or your mother-in-law, or your best friend may think. Go ahead—let him occasionally sleep in his street clothes, his undies, or his Halloween costume. It really doesn't matter that much.

Valerie Bell, Getting Out of Your Kids' Faces & Into Their Hearts

STRESSBUSTER #6

Breastfeed! And when you are nursing, look at feedings as an opportunity to sit down and rest—and enjoy the baby—rather than as another "task" to be completed. The prolactin rise that comes with breastfeeding works wonderfully to reduce stress.

J. S., mother of two, ages 12, 15

Worst Motherhood Advice I Ever Heard

"Take a bag of jelly beans with you on your trip. You can give them to your daughter when she's fussy." That is the perfect recipe for a hyper child and a stressful trip!

C. Y., mother of two, ages 2 months, 2

A Motherhood Stress Moment and How I Lived Through It

When our daughter was five, she was just coming into her independence. She loved to pick out her own clothes. In her five-year-old, fashion coordinator mind-set, the orange polka-dot dance leotard and yellow gingham bloomers went together perfectly with her mother's aerobic leg warmers—the maroon-and-white striped ones. She thought she had coordinated the perfect outfit for the first day of kindergarten. She couldn't understand how I thought differently.

After what seemed to turn into the third world war, something had to give. Her will was, by far, the strongest in the land and yet,

I was more than slightly determined that she was *not* going to school in those clothes!

I finally went to her closet and chose three outfits I could accept. I put them on the bed and told her to chose. She did and we were both happy. All she really wanted was a choice. And all I wanted was to save my dignity at the first parent-teacher conference!

I did find out later, however, she had worn the yellow gingham bloomers under her new school pants!

R. S., mother of three, ages 12, 16, 21

STRESSBUSTER #7

We didn't want to leave our new baby overnight. So my husband and I got a babysitter, went out to eat, and then got a hotel room for a couple of hours. It seemed like a crazy thing to do—but it was fun!

S. B., mother of three, ages 1, 3, 6

STRESSBUSTER #8

Get some help. You're not a bad mother if you get a babysitter so you can sleep or if you hire someone to help you clean house.

A. L., mother of one, age 1

STRESSBUSTER #9

Tell another mother what a good job she is doing with her children. You might start a trend.

Deborah

Worst Motherhood Advice I Ever Heard

"You'd better take that pacifier away from your baby."

How wrong! I learned to never take away something that provided comfort to a colicky, strong-willed child. She had her pacifier until thirty-five months, and it was worth the several hundred dollars in lost "pacies."

P. B., mother of two, ages 3, 5

STRESSBUSTER #10

When you feel irritable, anxious, or depressed, stop and ask yourself, What do I need right now? When you identify the need, plan a way to meet it. If taking care of your needs makes you feel selfish, remind yourself that you'll be a better mom if you give yourself the time to recharge and relax. You must give priority to your own needs, at least in some areas, at least occasionally.

Debbie Barr, A Season at Home

STRESSBUSTER #11

Don't obsess! Nobody does this parenting thing perfectly. Give yourself a break and don't dwell on mistakes or fears.

A. L., mother of one, age 1

STRESSBUSTER #12

Realize ahead of time that every day, by the end of the day, your *child* will do something *childish*. Decide that, with God's guidance, you will be the adult and will respond appropriately.

C. W., mother of three, ages 11 months, 2, 4

STRESSBUSTER #13

Think of your work as a mother as your job. This way of thinking helps me to better structure my day with a toddler and a baby. It also helps me to remember that the house and cooking and vacuuming are not the reasons I stay home. And it frees me to attend to the nurturing of my children.

L. S., mother of two, ages 20 months, 2

Worst Motherhood Advice I Ever Heard

"There are no accidents with children. Only a lack of parental forethought and planning." This from a government expert in accident prevention! Did this man ever know a two-year-old?

Deborah

A Motherhood Stress Moment and How I Lived Through It

When our youngest son was eight months old, he ate a caterpillar. His throat was embedded with the stiff, thorn-like hairs. He couldn't eat for almost a day. He cried a lot.

The doctors and poison control were stumped. One doctor suggested surgery to remove the burrs.

I called my mother and she came and took my older sons. My husband came home and he and I took turns holding the baby.

Finally I tried giving him papaya tablets—a mild digestive aid. Around midnight that night, the papaya had dissolved the caterpillar hair. He could eat again. Thank goodness!

R. K., mother of three, ages 8, 11, 14

STRESSBUSTER #14

Put shoes on small children and babies *after* you arrive at your destination.

J. S., mother of two, ages 2, 4

STRESSBUSTER #15

We need to realize that we have spiritual needs that only God can fill—our husbands cannot and our children cannot. We only add to our stress when we look to our husband and children to meet those needs.

Deborah

STRESSBUSTER #16

Pick your fights carefully. There will be disagreements galore while your child is growing up. Look at each situation and ask, "Will this decision matter in ten years?" If it will, stand your ground. If it won't, let your child make his or her own decision. (If the kid ends up with blue hair or a weird haircut, it will grow back.)

P. W., mother of one, age 17

Worst Motherhood Advice I Ever Heard ... on Toilet-Training

"Kids that aren't trained by two years old have something wrong with them."

P. H., mother of two, ages 5, 8

"Little girls are easier to train than boys." Ha!

M.W., mother of 2, ages 5, 7

"Boys should be toilet-trained by age two."

J. S., mother of two, ages 12, 15

"You can potty-train in one day."

A. P., mother of one, age 1

"Train her by taking her to the bathroom every hour." What a battle!

C. M., mother of one, age 3

"Go ahead and train your child!" Even though she was too young to realize she needed to go and couldn't get on the toilet herself or pull her pants down and back up.

C. M., mother of one, age 3

A Motherhood Stress Moment
and How I Lived Through It

Some of the most stressful times for me involved potty-training my three children. The hardest part was hearing how easily everyone else's children were trained—at nine months old. (Yeah, right!) I finally decided that as long as I wasn't sending Pampers to school in a bookpack, I didn't care when they were trained! (Come to think of it, I did send dry panties to school until second grade.) But, so what? They're children!

C. P., mother of three, ages 6, 12, 14

STRESSBUSTER #17

Establish daily rituals of affection—times every day when you stop to cuddle, tickle, or touch your child. These rituals can be anything! Hold him on your lap for a bedtime story. Cuddle when she gets up from her nap. Rock him to sleep. Rub her back while she tells you about her day at school. Then *guard* those times and don't let the busyness of life crowd them out.

Deborah

STRESSBUSTER #18

Get into a weekly Bible study that has decent child care. You will gain wisdom and encouragement, and you will build a network of Christian women to share and support you as a mother.

D. S., mother of four, ages 12, 16, 17, 19

STRESSBUSTER #19

Do not attempt to treat each of your children in the same way; they are each different people with different needs. Discover what those needs are and act accordingly.

Diane Eble, A Life You Can Love

STRESSBUSTER #20

Anticipate your children's needs. Before I'd take the baby into a store, I would sit in the car and nurse him so he wouldn't be hungry in the middle of shopping. Later I learned to start my grocery trip down the aisle that led toward the bathrooms. Then five to ten minutes into grocery shopping, I'd take my preschoolers into the restroom with me, and let the power of suggestion take care of that stress.

Deborah

A Motherhood Stress Moment and How I Lived Through It

Imagine a dreary fall day in Chicago. I had an infant and a two-year-old. The rain wouldn't stop. Our basement began leaking from the rafters and through the walls. Then a water pipe burst in the basement. And *then* the sewer backed up into the basement. I sat for the afternoon crying over it all. The baby cried too, and I couldn't quiet her.

I opened my eyes to see tiny white footprints going round and round on the dark rug. They were powder footprints—from the talcum powder my two-year-old had dropped in the bathroom. They reminded me of the cartoon, "Family Circus," and I began to laugh. I realized that the whole house could collapse—the important things were my husband and two girls.

My tears turned to laughter and I hugged my babies with a smile.

A. C., mother of three, ages 6, 10, 13

STRESSBUSTER #21

Get exercise—join an aerobics class, jog, walk, or do whatever appeals to you. Exercise produces more energy than it uses, and it promotes a feeling of control. I am amazed at the renewed sense of perspective I gain when I walk.

Deborah

STRESSBUSTER #22

Good mothers come in many styles. Know your style and build on your strengths. This can free you from the trap of comparing yourself to other moms.

Diane Eble, A Life You Can Love

Worst Motherhood Advice I Ever Heard

"The best policy when children make hurtful comments or sassy back talk is to ignore it."

This from my graduate school professor! Now I think my sons thought I didn't care what they said.

R. K., mother of three, ages 8, 11, 14

STRESSBUSTER #23

Choose advice wisely and trust your own instincts.

A.C., mother of three, ages 6, 10, 13

STRESSBUSTER #24

Don't waste your big guns on the little crises. Don't use the same tone of voice to say, "Comb your hair" as you would to say, "Don't lie."

Deborah Shaw Lewis, Motherhood Stress

Worst Motherhood Advice I Ever Heard

"Put the baby in a playpen so you can get things done."

My daughter hated it! And I couldn't stand hearing her cry.

M. F., mother of one, age 3

A Motherhood Stress Moment
and How I Lived Through It

We have found it helpful to give our children an allowance. They are required to give ten percent to our church and to save twenty percent. We do not replace any money that they lose and they may not ask us to give their allowance in advance. Other than that, the money is theirs to spend.

This is wonderfully freeing! If they want something—baseball cards, candy, to play a video game, a class ring—I can say, "It's your money, you decide." If they're broke before the end of the month, I can be sympathetic.

Recently our fifteen-year-old went on a four-day church youth trip. Other kids were bugging their parents to give them fifty or more dollars to take as spending money.

We just looked at our son and said, "How much of your money do you want to take?"

Then we gave him an extra $10, a gift from us. He was thrilled!

Deborah

STRESSBUSTER #25

Learn to tolerate a little (or a lot) more noise and confusion.

J. S., mother of two, ages 2, 4

STRESSBUSTER #26

Be free not to divulge to everyone all the details of your life and your problems with your child. Sometimes just say that everything is "fine."

Rosemarie S. Cook, Parenting a Special Needs Child

STRESSBUSTER #27

Allow your child to pay the consequences for making a bad decision. Do not always rescue him. Children learn valuable lessons when they are held accountable for their actions. There is a difference between rescuing them and offering them support.

R. S., mother of three, ages 12, 16, 21

STRESSBUSTER #28

Focus on the good stuff. When I'm overwhelmed, and my six-year-old wants something, it's easy to view him as another pressure. But if I take a moment to look into his eyes, smile at him, and remember that all too soon he'll be leaving for college—I can relax. And I focus on the joy of that moment—the sparkle in his eyes, his charming smile, the adoration on his face when he looks at me . . . and I talk to him, while I get him whatever he wanted.

Deborah

STRESSBUSTER #29

Don't sweat the small stuff!

S. T., mother of two, ages 6, 8

STRESSBUSTER #30

Enjoy every minute, even the small stuff.

S. T., mother of two, ages 6, 8

A Motherhood Stress Moment and How I Lived Through It

My seventeen-year-old daughter had a boyfriend—a real jerk. He wasn't overtly disrespectful, but it was there under the surface. I tried to be nice and treat him like I treated her other friends, but it was a struggle.

My mother advised me, "Don't tell her you don't like her boyfriend." That was tough. Then one day, my daughter *asked* me if I liked him. I thought for a moment and then told her the truth. She asked why and again I told the truth: I had a bad feeling about him, and she acted differently when she was around him.

Two weeks later she broke up with him. She told me later that after our talk, she watched for the things we had talked about. She then saw the disrespect, not only for adults, but also, in small ways, for her.

I guess the lesson in this is to always be honest with your children. My daughter knew she could trust me to tell the truth. And I hadn't nagged her about it, so she could hear what I said.

P. W., mother of one, age 17

STRESSBUSTER #31

Try a Huckleberry Day. The family gets in the car, but a child decides where the car goes, how money is spent, and if and when the family has lunch. It's like getting on Huck Finn's raft and adventuring with the stream. Originally I thought this would be a way to give a child a sense of power for a day. I didn't realize how much I would learn about my children's likes and dislikes, or what adventures we would have when my children were calling the shots.

Valerie Bell, Getting Out of Your Kids' Faces and Into Their Hearts

STRESSBUSTER #32

Go on a date with your husband regularly. Whatever that costs, it will be cheaper, less stressful, and better for your children than a divorce!

Deborah

STRESSBUSTER #33

I occasionally pay a babysitter to watch my daughter while I treat
myself to a full body massage.

L.G., mother of one, age 2

STRESSBUSTER #34

Set limits for your child that are reasonable and developmentally appropriate for his age. For example, don't expect a two-year-old to sit quietly in church.

C. H., mother of two, ages 12, 15

STRESSBUSTER #35

Buy some storytelling or humor tapes. Instead of listening to music as you travel, listen to comedy or stories and enjoy laughing together.

Deborah

Worst Motherhood Advice I Ever Heard
. . . on Babies

"You are going to starve that baby."

This from my mother every time she saw me breastfeed my baby.

R. F., mother of three, ages 17 months, 3, and soon-to-be newborn

"Just let her cry!"

My daughter had newborn colic for several months. I discovered that both she and I were happier if I held her.

J. T., mother of two grown children, two grandchildren

"Don't let your baby suck his thumb."

Ridiculous! Thumb-suckers are usually happy babies.

C.N., mother of two, ages 13, 15

"Make them walk early."

This friend actually had ways to force children to learn to walk. My children walked when they were ready. And it was *not* an indication of their intelligence!

K. V., mother of two, ages 2, 5

"You play with your baby too much."

This is *not* possible.

L. S., mother of four, ages 8, 10, 14, 16

A Motherhood Stress Moment
and How I Lived Through It

My daughter had "colic"—that thing that makes babies scream for, what seems to you and me, no reason at all. She screamed from sunup to sundown and well into the evening hours—fifteen to sixteen hours straight. This went on for several weeks, every day, every night, never fail.

I tried everything under the sun to pacify her: walking, talking, singing, rocking, bouncing, riding in the car. I even tried setting her carrier on the dryer. That worked periodically, but my dryer had a buzzer that went off when it quit and that ruined everything.

One day my husband arrived home at six o'clock to find me on the kitchen floor, sobbing relentlessly. I had not eaten all day, had not showered. The kitchen was a mess. Beds weren't made. There was no dinner on the table. I felt like I should have been holding a white surrender flag in my hand.

How could this bundle of joy I was supposed to love the rest of my life have gotten the best of me? No one had prepared me for this!

Thank God for my understanding husband. What I needed was a hug—and I got it. Then I knew it would be okay. My husband loved me. And I could praise God for him and for my child.

P. B., mother of two, ages 3, 5

STRESSBUSTER #36

Establish a daily quitting time at home, just as if you had a paid job. Of course, you can't go off duty as far as your children are concerned, but you can draw the line on housework and begin to attend to some of your own needs.

Debbie Barr, A Season at Home

STRESSBUSTER #37

When you become a parent, raising that child becomes your primary job. Don't worry so much about other responsibilities: job advancement, housecleaning, church work, etc. In good conscience let those things go and do a good job of parenting.

J. T., mother of two grown children, two grandchildren

STRESSBUSTER #38

I settled all the fights about who got to sit in the front car-seat by setting up a schedule. I even write it on my calendar. Each child has his week. And I take advantage of my time in the car, catching up on what is going on in that child's life.

Deborah

STRESSBUSTER #39

Most moms struggle at some point with the question of whether or not we have what it takes to meet the needs of our children. Adoptive moms can face unique challenges on this issue. In response to the questions that come, we can realize that each of us is divinely chosen to be the mother of each child under our care.

Elisa Morgan, Mom to Mom

STRESSBUSTER #40

Answer all your children's questions honestly. You don't need to go into details that the child didn't ask about. But if he is old enough to ask, he is old enough to receive a complete and honest answer. Even if the answer is "I really don't know."

P. W., mother of one, age 17

Worst Motherhood Advice I Ever Heard

"You should:

... wean your baby by twelve months"

... potty-train her by two years"

... enroll her in preschool by three"

Everyone wants your baby to grow up *fast*.

C. P., mother of three, ages 6, 12, 15

STRESSBUSTER #41

Look around until you find a good doctor—one who listens to you and supports your mothering style.

Deborah

STRESSBUSTER #42

It really helps to have some interest outside the home. I work part-time and that is always a breath of fresh air.

L. S., mother of two, ages 20 months, 2

STRESSBUSTER #43

Remind yourself that you are not perfect. Your husband isn't perfect. Your children won't be perfect. Let love be the undercurrent running through the times of frustration and turmoil.

P. B. mother of two, ages 3, 5

STRESSBUSTER #44

Get away every day for a little bit of alone, quiet time.

E. S., mother of two, ages 10, 15

STRESSBUSTER #45

Listen to music.

M. C., mother of two, ages 4, 6

STRESSBUSTER #46

Give your child positive attention *before* he or she demands it. Children can be persistent! They will get attention from you one way or another. Take care of their need for your time and attention first and they will be happy. And you can have some peace.

Deborah

A Motherhood Stress Moment and How I Lived Through It

One night I was trying to get supper on the table. My fourteen-month-old daughter kept fussing, wanting me to fill her cup with juice. But I didn't have a hand free to do that. Finally she asked again, and I told her to "hold your horses."

The next thing I knew, my toddler was dragging her rocking horse from the living room into the kitchen. That caught my attention!

I immediately picked up her and, laughing, gave her a hug. I found time to give her some juice. Then I finished supper in peace.

K. D., mother of two, ages 16, 18

STRESSBUSTER #47

Listen to your body. If you are tired, rest. If you are hungry, eat.

R. K., mother of three, ages 8, 11, 14

STRESSBUSTER #48

Accept the fact that every baby has her own personality from birth. You did not *make* her that way!

S. M., mother of two, ages 7, 9

STRESSBUSTER #49

Relax, relax, relax! If this is difficult for you, find a friend or two to talk with about all your baby troubles and other stressmakers. It helps to talk to someone else.

C. N., mother of two, ages 13, 15

Worst Motherhood Advice I Ever Heard

"Small children should be taught not to touch things. Breakable things *can* be left within reach of children. You only have to be firm with your child."

K. T., mother of two, ages 3, 7

A Motherhood Stress Moment
and How I Lived Through It

When our triplets were two-and-a-half to three-and-a-half years old, they were all at the stage of showing their independence—growing in so many ways. But they could not yet master the motor skills necessary to do the things they attempted. They'd become frustrated and give way to fussing and whining. Needless to say, that got on my nerves!

I found that even though I spent less time changing diapers and fixing bottles (which I had done so much of when they were smaller), we still needed a schedule. Each day went more smoothly if they knew—and I did, too—what was coming next. I concluded that children benefit from some structure as much as adults do.

M. H., mother of three 10-year-olds

STRESSBUSTER #50

When I'm stressed out, I remind myself that if something happened to my daughter, I'd wish for even the stressful times. I don't mean to be morbid, I just want to live each day with no regrets, realizing how precious, and short, my time with her will be.

C. M., mother of one, age 3

STRESSBUSTER #51

Always take the time to praise your child for the positive things she has done.

M. W., mother of two, ages 5, 7

STRESSBUSTER #52

Prepare for the chaos hours of late afternoon and early evening. Everyone in the family is hungry and tired by this time of day. And the rule seems to be that children are hungry a half hour before dinner is ready but somehow not interested in eating when it's on the table.

Rosemarie S. Cook, Parenting a Child with Special Needs

STRESSBUSTER #53

When you can, curl up in a blanket, read, and drink some hot tea.

K. V., mother of two, ages 2, 5

A Motherhood Stress Moment and How I Lived Through It

My three-year-old son seems to be into everything he shouldn't be—the pantry, putting things into the microwave, playing with the window blinds. He was being disciplined every day for the same things. He would always say, "I forgot!" So we put stickers on *everything* in the house that he wasn't allowed to touch.

It has helped a lot. But my house looks a little strange. We have stickers on the TV, VCR, stereo, blinds, pantry, refrigerator, stove, microwave, bathtub . . . even his baby sister's back.

R. F., mother of three, ages newborn, 1, 3

STRESSBUSTER #54

Material things are of little importance to small children. You can simplify and economize in planning parties, buying toys and clothes. The beauty of a birthday party to a child is that he or she is the center of attention and has friends and family and fun. Balloons and a homemade cake are as satisfactory as a bakery cake and a hired clown.

J. T., mother of two grown children, two grandchildren

STRESSBUSTER #55

Do something silly with your children. We were waiting for our new dryer to be delivered when I announced to our children that I had ordered a pink dryer with purple trim. We spent our waiting time thinking up sillier and sillier color combinations. What fun!

Deborah

STRESSBUSTER #56

Keep on and keep on trying to communicate with your teenage children.

E. S., mother of two, ages 10, 15

STRESSBUSTER #57

Take the children to a park and let them play. The housework and any other problems seem more manageable when you get home.

Deborah

A Motherhood Stress Moment
and How I Lived Through It

My first baby was a full-term baby. No health problems. But I had read so much about SIDS (Sudden Infant Death Syndrome) that I'd lie in bed all night, his cradle on the floor next to me, and listen to him breathe, ready to jump up if he didn't take his next breath.

After more than a week without ever really sleeping, I reached the end of my emotional rope. I broke down and prayed, "Lord, if you're going to take him, take him. I can't go on like this." And I finally went to sleep.

C. B., mother of two, ages 7, 11

STRESSBUSTER #58

Bring spontaneity back into your routine. On a clear summer
night wake your child and take her star gazing.

Elisa Morgan and Carol Kuykendall, What Every Mom Needs

STRESSBUSTER #59

When my daughter was a baby, I had trouble finding time to take a shower. So I bought a clear shower curtain. And I would put her in her infant seat on the bathroom floor, and she was happy watching me shower.

C. Y., mother of two, ages 2 months, 2

STRESSBUSTER #60

Don't try to give your children everything. Character is built by delaying gratification and by earning privileges and treats.

J. T., mother of two grown children, two grandchildren

STRESSBUSTER #61

When my teenage son is being defiant, I can reduce my stress by
backing off and giving him some space—and by offering him
choices that are acceptable to me.

C. H., mother of two, ages 12, 15

STRESSBUSTER #62

I like to go in my children's rooms when they've dropped off to sleep. I put my hand on their shoulder and pray, sometimes thanking God for something positive I saw that day. Other times praying about a concern. The nights I can do that, I go to bed with a better perspective and less stress.

Deborah Shaw Lewis, Motherhood Stress

Worst Motherhood Advice I Ever Heard

"The doctor knows what he is talking about—you should *always* take his advice."

B. O., mother of four, ages 1, 4, 19, 20

STRESSBUSTER #63

When stressed, I take a few deep breaths and remind myself of
how much I wanted this child, how hard I worked for it (a year of
fertility treatments), and of how happy I was to see that stick
finally turn blue!

A. T., mother of one, age 2

A Motherhood Stress Moment
and How I Lived Through It

When our daughter was little, we were told, "There is nothing wrong with your daughter's eyes!" This from a doctor, teachers, and the health department. For a year I tried to believe them, and I ignored my motherly instinct. I finally followed my heart and took her to an opthalmologist. Glasses were prescribed, and my child could finally "see straight." At last she could make her letters, tie her shoes, and cut a straight line.

A. C., mother of three, ages 6, 10, 13

STRESSBUSTER #64

Motherhood is a constant process of "letting go." It's a mother's nature to want to hold on and a growing child's nature to want to pull away. This creates stress. There has to be compromise and balance.

C. H., mother of two, ages 12, 15

STRESSBUSTER #65

Tell your child a story about when he was younger.

Deborah

STRESSBUSTER #66

Take a deep breath and say, "With God's help, I *can* handle this!"
R. F. , mother of three, ages newborn, l, 3

STRESSBUSTER #67

No matter what your childrens' ages, get to know their friends.

S. K., mother of three, ages 42, 47, 54

STRESSBUSTER #68

Getting our older child started in high school has been stressful! We've coped by getting to know the school by attending functions there, meeting teachers, and keeping the lines of communication open with our child. And, every morning, after he leaves for school, I pause and pray for him and his teachers.

J. S., mother of two, ages 12, 15

STRESSBUSTER #69

Quality time is NOT more important than quantity time. Both are essential! Quantity time gives you unplanned spontaneous opportunities for sharing and teaching about God. It is also important for the role modeling of family as a priority.

D. S., mother of four, ages 12, 16, 17, 19

Worst Motherhood Advice I Ever Heard

"Let your kids do as they please. They're only little once. They'll grow out of it."

D. B., mother of three, ages newborn, 6, 8

STRESSBUSTER #70

Find a prayer partner with whom you are comfortable praying over the phone. Nap times or early mornings are good times to connect with your prayer partner.

Debbie Barr, A Season at Home

STRESSBUSTER #71

Drop stressful outside activities and responsibilities for the first year or two you are a mother. Then gradually add back the things *you* miss the most.

C. W., mother of three, ages 1, 2, 4

STRESSBUSTER #72

Reconcile yourself: It does *not* get easier as they get older.

J. S., mother of two, ages 12, 15

STRESSBUSTER #73

Have one-on-one time with each child. It has been a challenge for us to find the time, but when we do, we are more able to understand and meet their needs individually.

M. H., mother of three 10-year-olds

STRESSBUSTER #74

Laughter may even promote healing. What a delightful tool for stress management! . . . It lights up our faces, relaxes our muscles, lowers our sense of vigilance, restores our objectivity, and enhances hope.

Norman Cousins, Anatomy of An Illness

STRESSBUSTER #75

Sign field trip forms and other school papers and send them back the next day.

Deborah

STRESSBUSTER #76

I've found it stressful to watch my children do something unwise—not knowing how to support them—wanting to let them know that we believe in them. I pray for them. And I remember that this is a learning exercise for them.

C. G., mother of three, ages 21, 26, 29

STRESSBUSTER #77

Children are resilient. Handle them with honesty and humor.
Elisa Morgan and Carol Kuykendall, What Every Mom Needs

STRESSBUSTER #78

Do something kind for someone else. Researchers call it "helper's high," the calm feeling of well-being that results from service to others.

Deborah

STRESSBUSTER #79

I've found that in disciplining my children, consistency—not severity—is the important thing. With children, punishment shouldn't be harsh. But they need to know that every time they break the rules, they will be disciplined—that's consistency. And if I'm consistent, they do not test limits as much. And that means a lot less stress for me.

L. G., mother of four, ages 4, 6, 11, 14

A Motherhood Stress Moment and How I Lived Through It

My seven-year-old son felt that our family spent too much time on his three-year-old sister. He often expressed resentment toward her.

I now get her favorite babysitter—or request extended time at day care—once a week. Then my son and I have a "date." We skate, swim, read, go to a movie, bike, go for ice cream, or whatever he wants to do. He gets to make the choice.

K. T., mother of two, ages 3, 7

STRESSBUSTER #80

When I know I've blown it, I try to admit my mistake and ask forgiveness if it is needed. Even from my husband and children. Then I also pray to God about it. Because I've found forgiveness to be a real stress reliever.

Deborah Shaw Lewis, Motherhood Stress

STRESSBUSTER #81

Learn your own limits. Save time and energy for your family, and say no to other demands.

S. T., mother of two, ages 6, 8

STRESSBUSTER #82

When your kids are teenagers, remember that a soft answer often turns away wrath.

E. S., mother of two, ages 10, 15

Worst Motherhood Advice I Ever Heard

"You absolutely *must* invite every child in the class to your child's birthday party."

C. M., mother of ten, ages 9 months–13 years

STRESSBUSTER #83

My sister and I have children the same ages. One day I called her and told her what my kids were doing to drive me nuts. She laughed and said, "How childish of them!" And I laughed too. That has gotten to be a joke between us. She calls me all stressed-out from some crazy thing her kids have done, and I tell her that her children are being *so* childish. That one phrase reminds us that they are, after all, just children. And when one of us says, "How childish!" we both laugh.

Deborah

STRESSBUSTER #84

Have your children do chores. They benefit by feeling needed and by learning how to do things. And you benefit by having some help. (They will, after a while, actually *be* a help.)

Deborah

STRESSBUSTER #85

I stopped trying to be superwoman. I cut back on my part-time job and started doing what I most love to do—reading to my children.

A. D., mother of two, ages 8, 10

STRESSBUSTER #86

With three teenagers and one preteen, my greatest motherhood stress is schedule exhaustion: late bedtimes, multiple activities for each child, meals, laundry, doctor visits, and so forth. I survive by praying a lot for strength and wisdom. And I *make* time to stay connected with my spouse. I try to be flexible. I laugh when I can. And I remember that they will be grown and gone all too soon.

D. S., mother of four, ages 12, 16, 17, 19

A Motherhood Stress Moment and How I Lived Through It

One Sunday, with my three young children in tow, I went to church feeling, and apparently looking, stressed. An older woman admonished me: "Cherish these days, dear. The years will go by so fast!"

Well, I wasn't having a day I wanted to cherish. So, when we got home I called my mother. "Mom," I said, "you had six children. Tell me. Do the years really fly by?"

My mother was silent for a moment. Then she replied, "Well, the years do go by fast. But some days last forever."

D.V., mother of four, ages 9, 14, 18, 21

STRESSBUSTER #87

Let your husband (or sister, or grandmother, etc.) help as much as possible. Someone besides mother can do a good job too.

M. H., mother of three 10-year-olds

STRESSBUSTER #88

When I deal with professionals, I approach meetings from a cooperative aspect. They are the experts in their field, I am the expert on my son, and we will work together in matching our collective wisdom to reach the best solution for whatever situation we are discussing.

Rosemarie S. Cook, Parenting a Child with Special Needs

STRESSBUSTER #89

I keep a copy of *Reader's Digest* in the car. When I have to wait for my children after school or whatever, I take a mini vacation. Instead of sitting there and thinking, Where are they? And why are they late? I think, This is a mini vacation. I have five whole minutes to read "Life in These United States."

D. V., mother of four, ages 9, 14, 18, 21

STRESSBUSTER #90

Make your preschool children rest. When our daughter was one, she wanted to give up her nap. I knew I couldn't make her sleep. But I also knew that she is easily overstimulated and needs her downtime. I required her to rest in her crib. Usually after playing for a few minutes she would fall asleep.

C. Y., mother of two, ages 2 months, 2

STRESSBUSTER #91

Two or three times a year, I get away for two days of R&R. My husband takes the children. And I go to visit a friend. I've even stayed alone in the home of a friend who was away.

A. D., mother of two, ages 8, 10

Worst Motherhood Advice I Ever Heard

"You don't spank them enough. If you did, they would mind."

This despite the fact my two sons have attention deficit disorder.

P. D., mother of two, ages 11,14

A Motherhood Stress Moment and How I Lived Through It

When our son was twelve years old, he pierced his ear. We decided that not saying anything would be the best response. So that night at dinner, nothing was said about the small earring in his ear. Nothing was said over the next few days.

A few days later, I noticed peroxide and cotton in our son's bathroom. Apparently, his ear had become infected. The earring was gone for good.

Some time later, he came home with his hair closely trimmed, except for one shock of hair falling over his forehead. He knew we didn't care for it, but we said little, other than requiring that it not cover his eyes.

One day he appeared at breakfast with his hair neatly trimmed. If we had nagged or harped at him, he might have kept it forever.

C. H., mother of two, ages 12, 15

STRESSBUSTER #92

When I've having a good day, I double my supper recipe and put the extra meal in the freezer. On a bad day, I can warm it up.

R. G., mother of four, ages 2 months, 1, 2, 4

STRESSBUSTER #93

Having a very good day? Triple your supper recipe. Serve one for your family, put one meal in the freezer. Then call a friend and offer her family the third meal.

Deborah

STRESSBUSTER #94

Watch "Mr. Rogers' Neighborhood" with your kids.
Elisa Morgan and Carol Kuykendall, What Every Mom Needs

STRESSBUSTER #95

Motherhood is undeniably stressful. But it's also an almost unimaginable honor and privilege. And I often remind myself of that with a ritual I began with my oldest son and have continued with all five of my children. From time to time I'll pull him aside, look deep into his blue eyes and tell him, "I'm the luckiest mama in all the world. Because of all the mamas in all the world and all the boys in all the world, God let me be your mama."

Deborah Shaw Lewis, Motherhood Stress

The MOPS Story

As a ministry of a local church, a MOPS group provides a caring, accepting atmosphere for today's mothers of preschoolers (infant through kindergarten). Here a mother has an opportunity to share concerns, explore areas of creativity, and hear biblically-based instruction that equips her for the responsibilities of family and community. The MOPS program also includes MOPPETS, a program providing a loving learning experience for children.

To find out if there is a MOPS group near you, or if you're interested in learning how to start a MOPS group in your community, please write or call: MOPS International, 1311 S. Clarkson St., Denver, CO 80210, 303-733-5353 / 800-929-1287

More Stressbusters for Moms

If you would like to share your motherhood stressbusters for another book, please answer the following and send to: *Stressbusters for Moms*, Zondervan Publishing House, Grand Rapids, MI 49530.

1. Imagine that you have a younger sister who has a new baby. If you could give her two pieces of advice—two bits of motherhood wisdom—what would they be?

2. What has been most stressful to you as a mother in the past year? What advice would you give a good friend on how to deal with that stress?

3. What was the worst advice on mothering anyone ever gave you?

4. Tell a short story about one time when you survived a stressful motherhood incident—big or small—or solved a motherhood problem.

name _____

phone number _____

address _____

number and ages of children _____